INVENTORS

GEORGE EASTMAN

PAUL JOSEPH
ABDO & Daughters

Published by Abdo & Daughters, 4940 Viking Drive, Suite 622, Edina, Minnesota 55435.

Cover illustration and icon: Kristen Copham
Interior photos: Bettmann, pages 5, 8, 23, 24, 27
                    Wide World Photos, pages 10, 13, 16
Photo colorization: Professional Litho

Edited by Bob Italia

Library of Congress Cataloging-in-Publication Data

Joseph, Paul, 1970-
    George Eastman / Paul Joseph.
    p.   cm. -- (Inventors)
    Includes index.
Summary: Sketches the life from poverty to riches of the inventor of the Kodak camera which made it possible for the ordinary person to take pictures.
    ISBN 1-56239-635-8
    1. Eastman, George, 1854-1932—Juvenile literature. 2. Photographic industry— United States—Biography—Juvenile literature. 3. Cameras—History [1. Eastman, George, 1854-1932. 2. Inventors. 3. Photography—History. 4. Cameras—History.]
I. Title. II Series: Inventors (Series)
TR140.E3J67 1996
338.7'61681418'092—dc20
[B]   95-51271
                                              CIP
                                               AC

Contents

The Camera

Every time you **pose** for a picture and say "Cheese," you can thank George Eastman. He invented the hand-held camera that we all use today.

Before Eastman, most people were not able to take pictures. Only those who had the right training and equipment could enjoy this expensive hobby.

The heavy camera was always placed on a **tripod**. Subjects had to stand very still for a long time while the picture was taken. If people moved just a little bit, the picture would come out blurry.

Eastman wanted to make **photography** easier— and he did. He invented a hand-held camera that everyone could use. Today's cameras are not much smaller than the one George invented in 1888.

Opposite page: A photographer under a black cloth, taking a picture of the Florida landscape.

Think of the pictures you and your family have taken. There are pictures of birthday parties, family get-togethers, fun vacations—even pictures taken underwater. George Eastman made it all possible.

It wasn't easy for George to make this invention. It took many hours of hard work—and almost all of his money. But he believed in his work, and made **photography** affordable for us all.

The Early Years

George Eastman was born July 12, 1854, in Waterville, New York. His father, also named George, died when young George was only eight years old. His mother, Maria, was left to care for George and his two sisters.

Times were tough for George and his family. His mother took in **boarders** to make money, but it was never enough. Often the family had oatmeal for breakfast, lunch, and dinner.

George promised his mother that he would work hard in school, get a good job, and take care of her. He told her he would some day fill her house with beautiful flowers.

George kept his promise and worked hard in school. He became one of the smartest students in his class and got excellent grades. George was especially good at math. At home he would help his mother with chores. In his spare time, he would read, often about **photography**.

By the time George was 13 years old, his family had no money. Sometimes they would go a day without eating. Although his mother didn't want George to quit school, George knew he was the man of the house. He had to get a job.

Thirteen-year-old George Eastman in 1867.

First Jobs

George became a messenger boy for an insurance company and made $3 a week. This kept food on the table for his family.

Because he was such a hard worker, his boss moved him into an office job within the first year. Now George made almost $9 a week. He could pay his bills and save some money.

With his savings, George bought his mother and sisters gifts. One gift he gave his mother was a photograph of himself. His mother loved it.

When he was 20, George used his math and organizational skills to get a job as a **bookkeeper** in a bank. He worked so many hours, his boss told him to relax and find a hobby. George decided to pursue his first love: **photography**.

Taking Pictures

George learned all he could about cameras. He decided to buy **photography** equipment and start taking pictures. Much to his surprise, he discovered that cameras weighed nearly 50 pounds (23 kg).

George had to use a wheelbarrow when he went into the countryside to take pictures. In those days, cameras were heavy. And they used **glass plates** instead of **film**.

Opposite page: This picture of the Genesee River in Rochester, New York, taken in 1877, is George Eastman's first-ever photograph.

Taking a picture was difficult. First, George set up a tent where he would **develop** the **glass plate.** Next, George set up the **tripod** on which rested the big, heavy camera. Then he would look for the picture he wanted to take.

Before the picture was taken, **chemicals** were placed on the glass plate. He would snap the picture and run to his tent to develop it before the glass plate dried. If it did, the picture was ruined.

Developing the picture was the hardest part of **photography**. Each picture took nearly an hour. And the process had to be done in total darkness. The smallest amount of light would ruin the plate. When the entire day was over, George often had only three pictures! But he enjoyed it.

Soon, all of George's free time was spent on photography. But he was tired of carrying the heavy equipment. There had to be a better way.

This illustration shows the equipment needed in the early days of photography.

Full-Time Inventor

George worked day and night on **dry plates** that could be **developed** at home. In 1880, he invented a machine that could make dry plates. He decided to quit his bank job and work full time on his new invention. He knew all photographers would want this dry plate machine.

In January 1881, George began the Eastman Dry Plate Company. Within one year, he was selling 4,000 plates a month.

Although business was good, the plates didn't always work. Sometimes they became foggy and the pictures would not develop. If only there was a way to take pictures without plates!

George Develops Film

George worked day and night on his new idea. He hardly ever slept. When he did, it was in his laboratory.

In 1883, George **developed** a thin strip of coated paper. He called it **film**. All the photographer had to do was wind the paper strip around a lightweight **spool** that could be fitted into any camera. It wasn't big, it didn't make a mess— and best of all, it produced wonderful pictures.

There was one problem: **professional** photographers liked the **dry plates**. They took pictures in their **studio** and did not worry about carrying heavy equipment. If George could build a lightweight camera that didn't use a **tripod**, he could sell it to almost everyone.

The Hand-Held Camera

For three years, George worked on his new idea. Finally, in 1888, he invented the first hand-held camera.

It was unbelievable! The camera didn't need a **tripod,** and it weighed slightly more than a pound. For $25, you received a camera loaded with **film**, a carrying strap, and a leather case.

Anyone could use George's camera. All the photographer had to do was aim, press a button, and the picture was taken!

When all the film was used, the photographer would send the camera to the Eastman Company. They would develop the pictures and return them with a new camera and film to the photographer.

Opposite page: Inventor Thomas Edison examines film developed by George Eastman.

George Eastman's

1854
George Eastman is born July 12th in Waterville, New York.

1862
George Eastman's father dies.

1867
Begins first job as a messenger boy for an insurance company.

1888
Introduces the simple box camera named the Kodak.

1891
Perfects daylight-loading film.

1892
Renames company the Eastman Kodak Company.

Detail Area

Life & Invention Timeline

<u>1874</u>
Eastman becomes a bookkeeper for a bank.

<u>1881</u>
Develops a process for making dry plates. Forms Eastman Dry Plate Co.

<u>1884</u>
Invents paperback film.

<u>1927</u>
Has a near monopoly on the photography business.

<u>1932</u>
Eastman dies March 14, in Rochester, NY.

* **Rochester**

* **Waterville**

New York

The Kodak

George bought a bigger **factory** and started making many cameras. There was only one problem: he had to convince people that they needed his new invention.

The camera needed a short, snappy name so people could remember it. The letter "K" was George's favorite, so he decided that the name would begin and end with "K." Then he tried many different letter combinations that made a word. Finally, he came up with the word "Kodak."

George placed ads in magazines and newspapers. They read: "Kodak cameras. You press the button, we do the rest."

The name and the ads worked. Everyone rushed out to buy a Kodak. Taking pictures became the new **craze** in America.

Keeping up with the camera demand was almost impossible. George now had three **factories** in New York with hundreds of people working day and night. He also built factories in London and Paris.

In 1891, George invented daylight-loading **film**. This new product allowed the photographer to reload the camera without using a darkroom. The new film made **photography** even more popular. In 1892, George renamed his company the Eastman Kodak Company.

George wanted everyone to enjoy photography. But he knew that some people could not pay $25 for a Kodak. So he designed the Bulls Eye which sold for $12. Then he invented the Falcon which sold for $5!

Still, George wasn't satisfied. As a child, he had loved cameras. But because he was poor, he could not buy one.

In 1900, George introduced the Brownie, a camera designed for children. It only cost $1. Soon, children everywhere were saving their money for a Brownie.

That same year, the Eastman Kodak Company moved into a new **factory** in Rochester, New York. It quickly became the city's major industry.

By 1927, Eastman Kodak was one of the nation's largest makers of photographic equipment. The company also had most of the country's **photography** business.

George Eastman (left) takes a picture of his good friend, inventor Thomas Edison.

George Eastman (center) with a group of friends on safari in Africa.

Promises Kept

George was now a **millionaire**. He had so much money he could do whatever he wanted. But all he wanted to do was build smaller and better cameras.

George began to work less. He loved going on vacations and taking pictures. He once went on an African **safari** and took pictures of zebras, elephants, and rhinos.

George always remembered his younger days when he was poor. He remembered how his mother tried to provide for the family, and how he made a promise to her. He kept that promise.

George built his mother a large house and filled it with the flowers and plants she loved. This made her very happy. She was proud of her son and his accomplishments.

But George didn't stop there. He quietly began sharing his wealth. He believed children had a better chance in life with good health. So, he set up dental **clinics** in Rochester, London, Paris, Rome, Stockholm, and Brussels. He also **donated** money to build a hospital.

Because he loved music, George established the Rochester **Symphony** and the Eastman School of Music. George's charity gained him much attention, so he started sending all his donations signed "Mr. Smith."

George Eastman died on March 14th, 1932. Not only was he a great inventor, he was a generous human being who helped make the world a better place to live.

Inventor George Eastman.

Glossary

bookkeeper - A person who keeps track of money and accounts in a business.

boarders - People who pay money to live in someone's house for a short period of time.

chemical (KEM-uh-kull) - Different kinds of simple matter, such as acids and gases.

clinic (KLIN-ick) - A place where people can get medical treatment.

craze - A short-lived, eager interest in something.

develop - A way of putting chemicals on a plate or film to bring out pictures.

donation (doe-NAY-shun) - A gift of money or help.

dry plates - Photographic glass plates that do not need chemicals to take a picture.

factory (FACK-tor-ee) - A big building where items are made by machines or by hand.

film - A roll or sheet of thin material covered with a coating that is changed by light to make photographs.

glass plates - A plate filled with wet chemicals that was used to make photographs before the invention of film.

millionaire (MILL-yun-air) - A person who has a million or more dollars.

photography (foe-TAH-gruff-ee) - The taking of pictures.

pose (POZE) - To hold your body still in one position while someone takes a picture of you.

professional (pro-FESH-un-ull) - Making a business or trade of something which others do for pleasure.

safari (suh-FAR-ee) - A journey or hunting trip to Africa. (Safari comes from an East African word meaning "a journey.")

spool - A cylinder of wood, metal, or plastic on which something is wound.

studio (STEW-dee-oh) - The workroom of a photographer.

symphony (SIM-foe-knee) - A large group of musicians (orchestra) that play music, made up of brass, woodwind, percussion, and stringed instruments.

tripod (TRY-pod) - A three-legged support or stand for a camera.

Index